Women of the West
Folk Songs & Cowboy Ballads

for Flute and Piano
Arranged by Jon Jeffrey Grier

Piano

LudwigMasters
PUBLICATIONS

Background Notes

In the soundtrack of the American West in the 19th Century, migrants, ranchers, miners, and frontiersmen whiled away long and tedious hours singing a wide assortment of ballads, cowboy songs, and other ditties. It was a rich oral tradition that was occasionally written down, and many melodic and textual variations were improvised. Women, however, were seldom represented. Here are a few such songs in which women were the central figures, most of which were strong women making their way in a man's world.

1. ***Fair Fannie Moore*** is a British murder ballad that found its way across North America to become a cowboy song. This rather gruesome narrative genre can include songs sung from the perspective of the murderer, the victim, or a third party; some express some sympathy for the killer. Fannie Moore has two suitors – one rich and one poor. She loves and marries the poor shepherd boy Henry and spurns the "haughty" Randell, who stabs her in revenge. Randall is hanged for his crime. Henry goes mad and is eventually buried next to Fannie.

> *Yonder stands a cottage, all deserted and alone;*
> *its paths are neglected, with grass overgrown.*
> *Go in and you will see some dark stains on the floor --*
> *Alas! it is the blood of fair Fannie Moore.*

Studio portrait of Belle Starr, probably taken in Fort Smith, early 1880's.

2. ***Belle Starr*** was born Myra Belle Shirley and educated at an elite school for girls where she was given lessons in piano and classical languages. Belle's family moved from Missouri to Texas in 1864, where she became acquainted with Jesse James, Cole Younger, and other outlaws. Through times spent in California, Oklahoma, and Texas, she took many lovers, many of them outlaws, eventually becoming an accomplished horse and cattle thief. In the late 1870's she married a Cherokee named Sam Starr; they were arrested multiple times for horse thievery and various other crimes. Belle Starr was shot to death by an anonymous assassin at age 41 in 1889. She became famous due to a dime novel, Bella Starr, the Bandit Queen, or the Female Jesse James, which fictionalized her life.

> *Eight lovers they say combed your waving black hair,*
> *eight men knew the feel of your dark velvet waist.*
> *Eight men heard the sounds of your tan leather skirt,*
> *eight men heard the bark of the guns that you wore.*
> *Belle Starr, Belle Starr, tell me where you have gone?*
> *Since old Oklahoma's sand hills you did roam?*
> *Is it Heaven's wide streets that you're tying the reins,*
> *or single footing somewheres below?*

3. ***Flora, Lily of the West*** is a traditional British and Irish folk song. In the American version a man travels to Louisville and falls in love with a woman named Flora (or Mary or Molly), the eponymous Lily of the West. He catches her being unfaithful to him, and in a fit of rage stabs the man she is with, and is subsequently imprisoned. In spite of this, he finds himself still in love with her.

> *The trial was held, I made my plea, but 'twas of no avail,*
> *now I await the hangman in a stinkin' rotten jail.*
> *But though I give my all away, and though my life is messed,*
> *I love my faithless Flora, the Lily of the West.*

4. **Sweet Betsy from Pike** was first published in an 1858 songbook called **Put's Golden Songster**, which featured songs dealing with the 1849 California gold rush. It is based on an Irish melody that most likely came to the U.S. during the potato famine. There is a Pike County in both Missouri and Illinois from where many California-bound gold seekers began their land journeys. Many, many verses exist, making very different endings possible – foreboding (arriving in Hangtown, renowned for the number of hangings there), bitter (Ike & Betsy get divorced), or happy and domestic (they have 13 children, all named George). But in all, Betsy comes across as a strong and independent woman.

Now don't you remember sweet Betsy from Pike,
who crossed the big mountains with her husband Ike?
With two yoke of oxen, a big yeller dog,
a tall Shanghai rooster and one spotted hog.

They got a place down in the Columbia Gorge,
and had thirteen children that they all named George.
Now Betsy did the farmin' and huntin' while Ike
chased the thirteen sweet babies of Betsy from Pike.
Singing too ra li, loo ra li, loo ra li ay.

5. **Oh, My Darling Clementine:** Multiple variations of this song exist, but all center around Clementine, the daughter of a "miner forty-niner" and the singer's lover. One day while performing routine chores, Clementine trips and falls in the water and drowns, as her lover is unable to swim and unwilling to attempt to rescue her. The lyrics were written by Percy Montrose in 1884, based on an earlier song called "Down by the River Liv'd a Maiden". The origin of the melody is unknown. It has been claimed that the melody was from an old Spanish ballad made popular by Mexican miners during the California Gold Rush. Here the melody is mostly changed from its original 3/4 to 4/4 in the spirit of a lament.

A cowgirl, circa 1909.

Oh my Darling, Oh my Darling,
Oh my Darling Clementine.
You are lost and gone forever,
Dreadful sorry, Clementine.

6. **The Yellow Rose of Texas:** The first recorded copy of this folksong was handwritten on a plain piece of paper about 1836; this copy was most probably transcribed either shortly before or after General Sam Houston lead his brigade of Texas loyalists against the army of General Antonio Lopez de Santa Anna at the Battle of San Jacinto on April 21, 1836. The lyrics tell of a black American (presumably a soldier from Tennessee) who left his sweetheart (a "yellow rose") and yearns to return to her side. "Yellow" was a term given to Americans of mixed race in those days, most commonly mulattos. And "Rose" was a popular feminine nineteenth century name; frequently used in songs and poems as a glorification of young womanhood. There is some thought that the Yellow Rose of Texas was one Emily West, who had been captured to be a concubine by Santa Anna; supposedly, she distracted him in bed, giving Sam Houston the element of surprise in his attack.

She's the sweetest rose of color this darky every knew;
her eyes are bright as diamonds, they sparkle like the dew.
You may talk about dearest May and sing of Rosa Lee,
but the yellow rose of Texas beats the belles of Tennessee.

For my beloved in-house flutist, December 2020
Jon Jeffrey Grier, Arranger

About the Composer

Jon Jeffrey Grier holds a B.A. from Kalamazoo College, where he studied composition with Lawrence Rackley, an M.M. in Composition from Western Michigan University, studying with Ramon Zupko, and an M.M. in Theory and a D.M.A. in Composition from the University of South Carolina, where he studied with Jerry Curry, Dick Goodwin and Sam Douglas. Jon taught Advanced Placement Music Theory and Music History at the Greenville Fine Arts Center, a magnet school of the arts in Greenville, SC from 1988 to 2019, where he was named Teacher of the Year three times. Awards include grants from ASCAP, the Surdna Foundation, the South Carolina Music Teachers Association, the Metropolitan Arts Council, and the Atlanta Chamber Players. Jon has also been a writer/keyboardist in various jazz & fusion ensembles since 1984. He lives in Greenville with wife Marion and manic mongrel Roxanne.

WOMEN OF THE WEST
FAIR FANNIE MOORE

Traditional
arranged by Jon Jeffrey Grier

BELLE STARR

Traditional
arranged by Jon Jeffrey Grier

50410006

FLORA, LILY OF THE WEST

Traditional
arranged by Jon Jeffrey Grier

Women of the West
Folk Songs & Cowboy Ballads

for Flute and Piano
Arranged by Jon Jeffrey Grier

Flute

WOMEN OF THE WEST

FAIR FANNIE MOORE

Traditional
arranged by Jon Jeffrey Grier

50410006

3

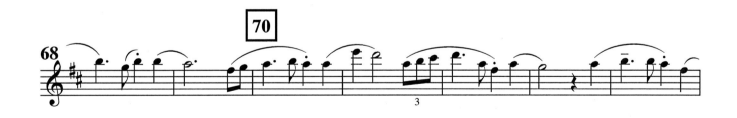

50410006

BELLE STARR

Traditional
arranged by Jon Jeffrey Grier

50410006

FLORA, LILY OF THE WEST

Traditional
arranged by Jon Jeffrey Grier

50410006

SWEET BETSY FROM PIKE

Traditional
arranged by Jon Jeffrey Grier

OH, MY DARLING CLEMENTINE

Traditional
arranged by Jon Jeffrey Grier

50410006

THE YELLOW ROSE OF TEXAS

Traditional
arranged by Jon Jeffrey Grier

50410006

SWEET BETSY FROM PIKE

Traditional
arranged by Jon Jeffrey Grier

OH, MY DARLING CLEMENTINE

Traditional
arranged by Jon Jeffrey Grier

THE YELLOW ROSE OF TEXAS

Traditional
arranged by Jon Jeffrey Grier

50410006

Selected Flute Publications

METHODS

BAKER, JULIUS
Cox, Alan

10300130   Daily Exercises for the Flute (Grade 4)
A terrific and valuable collection of exercises for advanced flutists, the studies in this book are intended to build a high degree of technical solidity by means of intensive work on scale, scale patterns, seventh-chord progressions, thirds, sixths, chromatic sequences, fast staccato, high tones, and various duet selections. By diligent and careful work on these daily exercises, students will build a flawless tehcnical foundation on the flute, and more advanced players will keep themselves in shape.

COLLECTIONS

BALENT, ANDREW

50341003   Classical Solos (Grade 2.5)

HARRIS, FLOYD O.

50341006   Competition Solos, Book 3 Flute (Grade 3.5)
A practical collection of competition solos for young instrumentalists, many of which are on state festival lists. The piano book includes alternate accompaniments for instruments of different pitch and therefore can be used for any instrument in the book three series. Titles included: Brass Bangles; Caprice; Dancing Silhouettes; Evening in the Country; Ocean Beach (Valse); Polka from Bartered Bride; Viennese Sonata No. 4 (Rondo)

HARRIS, FLOYD/ SIENNICKI, EDMUND

50341005   Competition Solos, Book 2 Flute/Oboe (Grade 2.5)
Book 2 is a practical collection of competition solos, many of which are on state festival lists. Piano book includes alternate accompaniments for instruments of different pitch and therefore can be used for any instrument in the book two series. Titles included: The Young Prince; Viennese Sonatina No. 1 (Allegro); Flower of the Orient; The King's Jester; Two Short Pieces; Spirit of Victory; Barcarolle and Scherzetto; Sparkles; Waltz from Album for the Young.

KERKORIAN, GREGORY M.

50341008   Easy Orginal Flutes Duets and Trios
Beautifully written and arranged with the young player in mind, these duets and trios make wonderful concert and festival repertoire for early performance.

SOLO, UNACCOMPANIED

ADLER, SAMUEL

10410523   Canto XIII for Flute (Grade 4)
Adler, Samuel. Published by Ludwig Music, Cleveland,. Copyright 1994. A rare piece for solo piccolo, this work may be performed straight, or the player may make dramatic entrances and theatrical gestures.

FERROUD, PIERRE OCTAVE

M284891   Three Pieces

SIENNICKI, EDMUND J.

10340101   Recorder Fun (Grade 1)

SOLO WITH PIANO

BACH, J.S.
Marteau, Henri

10410234   Andante Cantabile (Grade 3)
Andante Cantabile [Sinfonia Concertante in E-flat for Two Violins and Orchestra: Andante]

BRICCIALDI, GIULIO
Davis, Albert O.

10410186   Carnival of Venice for Flute and Piano (Grade 4)
This famous melody in theme-and-variations form features a marvelous cadenza. Its technical challenges are dazzlingly impressive!

BUSSER, HENRI

M114291   Petite Suite

M298091   Prelude Et Scherzo

CASELLA, ALFREDO

M266891   Barcarola E Scherzo

M371291   Sicilienne and Burlesque

CHAMINADE, CECILE

M114791   Air De Ballet: Seren

DEBUSSY, CLAUDE

M168591   Clair De Lune

GANNE, LOUIS

M127091   Andante Et Scherzo

GAUBERT, PHILIPPE

M186691   Deux Esquisses

M122791   Nocturne Et Allegro

M196191   Sicilienne: Madrigal

M218391   Sonata In A

M297991   Suite (Grade 4)
This suite, by renowned French flutist Philippe Gaubert, is in four movements, with each movement dedicated to a master flutist of the time. It is a fine contest or recital selection for the advancing musician. Movements: I. Invocation (danse de pretresses), II. Berceuse Orientale, III. Barcarolle, IV. Shzerzo-Valse

GERMAN, EDWARD

M330491   Suite

GLIERE, REINHOLD

M330691   Two Pieces, Op.35

GRIFFES, CHARLES TOMLINSON

M282291   Poeme

HAHN, REYNALDO

M342491   Two Pieces

HARTY, HAMILTON

M292591   In Ireland

HUE, GEORGES

M152191   Fantaisie (Grade 4)
Composed for the Paris Conservatory 1913 and later orchestrated in 1923, Hue's Fantasie is a beautiful work for the advancing flutist. The piece begins with a spacious and atmospheric Assez lent section, which is complimented by intricate melodic lines on the flute. This introduction leads into a beautiful Modere section and concludes with a rousing Tres vif encore.

REINECKE, CARL

W100891   Concerto Op. 283

ROSENHAUS, STEVEN

P001791   Rescuing Psyche
Rescuing Psyche for flute and piano was commissioned by the Music Teachers National Association and the NYSTMA and was premiered by flutist Kelly J. Covert and pianist Nathan Hess. Rescuing Psyche takes its inspiration from Greek mythology. Eros, a god, and Psyche, a mortal, are in love, but Aphrodite is jealous. Aphrodite successfully traps the mortal in a coma, but Eros wakes his love by playing a flute. The flute part has some key clicks and flutters but no other extended techniques or special effects are required.

WIDOR, CHARLES-MARIE

M183591   Suite, Op. 34

TRIO

KOECHLIN, CHARLES

M333291   Three Divertissements

Exclusively Distributed by

Alfred Music
LEARN · TEACH · PLAY

Questions/ comments? info@keisersouthernmusic.com